The Portage Poetry Series

Series Titles

Sparks and Disperses
Cathleen Cohen

Holding My Selves Together: New and Selected Poems
Margaret Rozga

Lost and Found Departments
Heather Dubrow

Marginal Notes
Alfonso Brezmes

The Almost-Children
Cassondra Windwalker

Meditations of a Beast
Kristine Ong Muslim

Praise for
Cathleen Cohen

Writing with indirection, delicacy and deep affection, Cathleen Cohen is an artist who trusts the free hand and the unplanned, the poem's gradual reveal toward what it harbors. In the felt presence of the unspoken, these sensitive, compassionate and soft-spoken poems, their subtle shades glowing many-hued, are suffused with light like the watercolors that are her other medium of finding the world again, the beauty of what's fleeting, the iridescence of things, the energies of what "sparks and disperses."

—Eleanor Wilner
author of *Before Our Eyes: New and Selected Poems, 1975–2017*

Sparks and Disperses touches reality and by this actual touching, reveals life in its exquisite brilliance and raw distress. Lines in these poems are delicate and robust; the superb brushwork of a poet whose heart & hand paint what John Keats would recognize as the joining of beauty with the truth of the imagination. Cathleen Cohen's life and poetry are a passionate expression of dedication to everything we need to live whole and meaningful lives.

—John Fox
The Institute for Poetic Medicine

Sparks

— and —

Disperses

Poems by

Cathleen Cohen

Cornerstone Press
Stevens Point, Wisconsin

Cornerstone Press, Stevens Point, Wisconsin 54481
Copyright © 2021 Cathleen Cohen

www.uwsp.edu/cornerstone

Printed in the United States of America.

Library of Congress Control Number: 2021943931
ISBN: 978-1-7333086-8-7

Cornerstone Press titles are produced in courses and internships offered by the Department of English at the University of Wisconsin–Stevens Point.

DIRECTOR & PUBLISHER   EXECUTIVE EDITOR   SENIOR EDITORS
Dr. Ross K. Tangedal   Jeff Snowbarger   Lexie Neeley & Monica Swinick

SENIOR PRESS ASSISTANTS
Claire Hoenecke

STAFF
Rosie Acker, CeeJay Auman, Shelby Ballweg, Megan Bittner, Kala Buttke, Caleb Feakes, Emma Fisher, Camila Freund, Kyra Goedken, Brett Hill, Adam King, Gavrielle McClung, Pachia Moua, Annika Rice, Alexander Soukup, Bethany Webb, Maggie Weiland

For
Tiffany Silliman Cohen
and Rabbi Gila Colman Ruskin

Also by Cathleen Cohen

Etching the Ghost

Camera Obscura

Contents

Sip This Vastness

Maybe a Hawk

Light Perceived in Reverse

Scatter All We've Claimed

Reaching for Shards

Logic I Must Learn

Sip This Vastness

When We Enter the Story

We may grasp
            fragments

that fall into our hands,
countless bits
swirling around us, a nonstop

flood. No need
to solder them together with gold
like kintsugi.

They already glitter
              from the time   presence
contracted
and poured into vessels,
                  which cracked.

We didn't witness the explosion.
But sometimes

don't you feel tremors?

Why I Paint at Dawn

The sky is a tint of violet,
delicate cloth.

There is a haze of cicadas
clicking their short lives out.

I crave the particulars:

finch flit
          from leaf to leaf,
branches expanding their reach.

I feather quick strokes
of lapis and topaz, bright

as gems on holy books.

Pomegranate

Bursts in my hand,
shooting fractured light
beyond skin.
Speaking to my children,
I break off, lost
in sea sounds,
calm Gulf of Aqaba, tides off Jaffa.
A thousand bird arias
boil out of the valley.
Simmering trees.
I startle
to see my hands
fashioning dinner,
slicing plums' flesh.
Seeds scatter
when I move.

As Far As

Green almonds salt the tongue.
Lilac air. Anemones cock red ears
above a thicket of figs.

Petals flame on shrubs
whose names no one recalls,
they are so plentiful.

We work the fruit groves,
pruning, looping hoses,
kneeling in stones.

I follow my sauntering cousins
into sweet grass,
taste of licorice.

But at night, jackals forage.
We check the chickens
in their pens

and crouch on outcrops
to gaze as far as
the Galilee Sea.

Suad and Her Daughters Sleep on the Porch

*"Let there be an expanse in the midst of the water, that it may
separate water from water."*
    —*Genesis* 1:6

They rouse at dawn
to olive groves and valleys
hazy with heat.
Trees shake out their tresses.

Sky oscillates like a great sea
creating its blues.
Cobalt rises from rock beds,
manganese glints in the shallows.

The women shake their mattresses
of dust and visions,
sea flowers and coral
they've never seen.

From here they could dive
down into the village.
But who would pull them from the waves
and lift them over the hull?

Wedding Season

From my roof the village glows,
a wavering necklace
of fragments, flung out.
Melodies thrum over Mt. Meron,
where sages are buried, old men
who once came out to dance at dusk.

These are not their songs.
Tonight a wedding bangs its drum.
Men shoot bullets into night's soft skin.
So many days preparing the feast,
slaughtering lambs. Hundreds to feed:
mangoes, baklawa, pickle, stuffed gourd.
White shirted men dance in a line,
women trill blessings.

I leave my roof, bound for Peqin
to pin a gift to the groom's lapel,
to greet the shimmering bride.
Another wedding cries out in full voice
past bones of sages, who stir
and share this sharp joy.

Outsider

Will she accept me,
outsider, new teacher?

I would offer a hand, but wait
and receive her stiff smile.

Like branches we tremble.
Her scarves twirl and unfurl.

As if on cue, we lean
to enfold each other,

two still women on the bright lawn
among cypresses.

I've brought a book for the children,
she holds out a plate of figs.

The air exhales in various languages,
embracing us.

Like Sweets

Samir writes of ascending fire clouds,
something he saw or dreamed.
We pause to think of it.

The first day hangs heavy.
August trails us into the school,
sky streaked azure.

We write poems, retracing days.
The children gaze, rapt
as I weave among them,

not wearing a hijab
as their teacher does, sentry
at her desk. Yet she laughs

at what jumps from their pens:
cotton clouds, slices of green,
words like sweets.

Writing Poems in Beersaba'h

Mahmood's name contains two mountains.
Modaefa's heart holds his brother and his horse.
I stare at limestone roads
which gird this city. His horse?

Nothing alters on him,
not a smile, not a flicker.
He lives far out and what do I know
of all he knows?
The color of his horse?

How he fares in thick rains
that pound the desert
or dust that streams in from Africa,
choking blue from the sky?

Does he finish his homework by flashlight?
Walk kilometers to the bus?
February heat blows through windows.
Students fill spaces.

They want to learn English and I yearn
to sip this vastness,
to touch Modaefa's horse and learn
why Ameen was named for patience
and Alaa, for prayer.

I want to sniff the exact bloom
Yasmeen was named for.

Lakiya

Salim and Nardeen prepare a feast,
a gleaming table. Their sons waver
among us for moments, then slip
to the sand beneath our chairs.

The boys ignore our sighs
over squash and sweet lamb.
Toy trucks shift gears over rugs
on the road to Beersaba'h.

Wheeling outside on bikes,
they widen the circle
past camels and prickle bush.

I strain to hear stories,
six cousins to a dorm room,
sharing the village's one suit,
that first year Bedouin were allowed
to enter classrooms.

We savor fresh baked flan,
green apricots, baklawa.
Night is fragrant with jasmine.

Salim snaps sprigs of verbena and lemon leaf,
herbs he brews each day at school.
He wants me to learn
their names and healing properties,
which I won't recall,

intent as I am
on pulsing stars, the sweep
of night birds and shouts of his sons
who race beyond the garden.

Marzuk's Jewels

He invites us to harvest the figs,
so we rise when the sky is a dark bowl
above the school.

We slip down the snake road
while villages doze:
Rama, Beit Jan, Peqin.

Marzuk's jewels are two dunams of vines,
olive trees and plum
nestled among rocks.

His elders knew the endless winds
that scour these hills,
that whistle through bones.

We follow the wadi to his truck,
where he offers the first taste,
sharp as a rose.

Reaching for fruit,
we comb through leaves
that surrender their nectar.

Not far from here, tomorrow
a gunman will board a bus and burst
the sky, so willing to pour its blood,

not the blush of this dawn
where we stand,
wiping juice from our lips.

Galilee Roses

Hot winds scour gardens,
squalls etch the hills.
Roses stand on stiff, thorned feet
among jagged rocks.

Women at windows
beat dust from their rugs
and flick pale hands in greeting
or warning.

The roses take weeks to open.
I set out my paints, eager
for them to unfurl
before the wind bares its teeth.

Once bloomed, the flowers survive
a day, two at most.
Crimson frills whip away,
a failure of shelter.

How we nurtured them,
knowing full well
that everything scatters
and soon, even the last petal.

Maybe a Hawk

Hidden

There's no sign, just silver numbers
on a close-mouthed door near Sam's Mufflers.
Second story walk-up, could be
the office of a lawyer or notary.
I hesitate on the stairs.

Murmur of prayers.
The principal appears, relieved.
First greet the parents, who rise
to offer cakes and sweet chai.

No resisting. They'd fix nicer snacks
but have no kitchen.
A search is on for a new sanctuary,
but they've had problems.

I'm led to a back room with locked doors,
blank walls, no books in evidence.
Children wait like candles,
ready to be lit.

Spilling papers and pens to the floor,
I ask for names and gather them in.

Ritual

If, upon waking, you tape to your feet
sticks of roasted willow,
you will draw the day's boundaries.

Glide across floorboards
to check at the window for rain
or dove flight.

You can slither down steps
as you race for the bus,
not pausing for shadows.

And the day will be so marked,
charcoal smudges under tables,
loop-de-loops through doorways,

thick lines where you stand
and where you fly,
bright filaments.

Art Project

Girls scatter like petals across a rug.
They glue paper mosaics
on a wide, white board.

Collaging bamboo walls and citrus groves,
they letter calligraphy in the borders.

Parrots loop through the tropics,
boys race to the mosque door,
late for noon salat.

One girl sighs and quickly
covers the boys with patterned squares.
It's unseemly to draw humans.

How the children brighten
this factory town of brickworks, fields
and a fear of strangers.

We snap photos but shield the girls.
Only their fingers protrude
from diaphanous veils.

Eclipse

We try not to stare
as orbs cross the sky
                 too close,
                 too intimate.

It's like spying on lovers
granted   only a brief touch.

Birds flit into hedges, warning
of chaos, dusk at midday.

Sharing filters and dark glasses,
we permit ourselves

quick glances, recalling
Icarus,
        hubris, wax wings,
                  plummeting.

Children weave among us, flirting,
lifting into handstands.

Perhaps we're here

not to monitor the sky,
but to watch them,
pull them to the ground.

Ink Drawings

Clouds under wrists.
Swallows tilt and change formation,
sweep at exhale,
roll into mist.
Spine
snakes down.
Invisible dogs wait,
haunches to the floor,
ears cocked.

Dance

with hands in mittens.
Space is a cavern.
Air blossoms
into trout-shaped flames
of moss and silver.
Ward off monsters
with a cotton sword.
Hands wing up.

Portents

Marcus shows how much
he doesn't want to be here,
growling, snapping pencils,
facing off with taller boys,
equally thin-skinned.

Threats roil the room.
Boys kick chairs, dissatisfied
with small explosions.
I grasp Marcus,

who exits royally,
one up on his rivals.
He admits that reading is mad joy
for the stickers, shiny stars
we paste to his shirt.

All he must do
is sit for twenty minutes
with hard words.
He tries to charm me (when uncertain)
but sounds them out.

Jittery legs. He scans
where boys prowl the halls,
mouthing

Gonna get you.   Later.

Another Child Can't Read

His spine curls
in rebellion, bent
like a loaded trap.

Fingers hide scratches
on papers and arms
no one may touch.
Hair shields eyes, hot stones.

I stand to the side
and whisper a few soft words,
imitating the wind.
I know this glint

from mining others' affections,
how to float above
sharp words,
to slow my approach

but draw close again and again,
as if circling a mountain
of cirrus clouds
that might evanesce.

Cortisol

A door slams open
like a bullet crack, too close
to our chairs in this tight, dim hall.

Keisha and I jump up from our books;
we're possum or fox, pricking our ears
for the next shot.

Seventh graders swarm from class.
Two boys eye each other, duck and twist.
The crowd shouts,
Pop him! Pop him!
This is better than YouTube.

Throwing punches, the boys
look scared. One checks
the ceiling for possible exit.

I've grabbed Keisha and dragged us
to the wall, which offers
little shelter.

Maybe a Hawk

Last week, a box of bullets
appeared

beneath a fourth grader's desk.
The children say

it fell from the sky,
or maybe a hawk dropped it.

Equations

Karim won't read equations,
just tears pages in his binder.
He is angry at God,
who has grown incomprehensible,
striking trees, drying rains
before they reach their streams.

Last week two boys held his flailing arms
and a third one punched.
Scurry of legs, slammed lockers,
no teacher, fractured air,
he on the cold floor.

His parents speak of it
in careful English to the principal,
in Urdu laments at home.
No one says racial, but God subtracts,
abandoning his creatures.

At the mosque he won't pray,
only slumps on a wall.
Soon he will refuse to go,
though his father shouts,
his mother weeps into her scarves.

It's not the red words hissing
through halls, through air,
but what he's learned of the deer
at water's edge, ears cocked
for any small click.

Guidance

The lock to the mosque door is stuck,
so Huda slips from her father's car
into mine, releasing her veil,

displaying long, tethered braids
I've never seen. She says
it's no problem, two females.

And the car provides an extra layer
from the outside. Her name
in Urdu means guidance.

She and her cousins taught me
how to wind a loose hijab,
pull it up and over like a lid

to enter sacred spaces.
How shocked they were
that first day I arrived, choking

in a tight, wool scarf.
They laughed and unknotted it
then grasped my hands.

Today a vee of geese skims the sky.
Huda confides of hundreds
where she lived.

She'd follow them down to the lake
where they'd drop clams.
Curling in the grass, she'd wait

until they departed
then cup pale butterfly shells.

Fathoms

On mornings this murky
there's nothing to do but swim
in oceanic air.

Wrapped in chlorine tides,
I'm queen of the pool, gracious
when a sea turtle swipes
with rough flippers. He's gruff,
bleary through goggles,
thrown off his laps.

But I am beneficent,
seeking the slick rush of grasses
and seaweed uncoiling
in dark, impossible greens.

Mysterious fish with spiked jaws
and luminous skin
circle much closer than we
to the heart of the world.

In the depths they trace
paths without stars,
atmosphere we don't know,
but crave.

Ecosystem

Teacher passes out pebbles.
Lamond slips one under his shirt.
He likes the sharp, little pressure that almost hurts.
An ecosystem of living things
working together.

Teacher sets out tall glass jars on a table
and tells everyone to gather around
but he won't. She shouts
for him to get up,
but he pretends to sleep.

They watch a video
on how pebbles and stones
might come from anywhere,
wash in from the sea or fall to earth
from exploding meteors.
Lightning bolts run through his.

They count off for partners.
He's supposed to work with Neesa
but doesn't like to leave his desk
and will fight if he has to.

Neesa eye-rolls then dumps
handfuls of pebbles into their jar,
then dirt, then the plant.

Teacher left them overnight
in the trunk of her car
so they look frozen,
but she thinks they will live.

Lamond draws himself
floating to the ceiling.
He doesn't need feet, maybe
wheels or suction cups.

Drawing Maps

The third graders are mapping
the neighborhood.
Nothing too complex, warns Mr. Joe.
It takes time to trust a pencil,
not grip it too tight.

They rarely draw and lack confidence.
He makes them slide fingers
up to the eraser and raise arms
like hinges, like gulls' wing.

Lately it's rare to sight seagulls,
but not unheard of.
He used to watch them coast
over the skyline like twists
of cotton or kite tails.

These city streets are grids, he says.
This will help you learn what's north, what's east,
the rough, gray river
that the children claim

they've never seen.
If he could take them to the roof,
they'd sketch tarnished waters,
lit blue through cloud breaks.

He reads them tales of the Lenape,
who lived here without maps,
divining the moods of the creeks
as they emptied and swelled.

The children do feel something.
He can tell by their bright drawings
of play lots, row homes and trees
springing up in the middle of the street.

Shimmer Around Us

An elder arrives for afternoon prayers,
perplexed that the entrance to the mosque won't budge,
but the school is on lockdown.
Teachers watch behind slit blinds,
finally releasing the door
so children spill into the street like flowers
emptied from a vase.
Jumping sidewalk cracks,
they are daisies seeding junked lots,
waving above fences.

Is this safe? Has enough time passed?
Sirens circle like wolves,
choking Ramadan's peace.
Five blocks away some boys blasted a cop.
Words ignite the street. No one knows
who was detained and
who now roams the alley with an injured heart.
They used birdshot
but few birds perch down here.

I gather my class with swooping arms.
We will need to write poems
about everything that shattered today:
fractured air, bruise-dark sky,
the few shards of light
that shimmer around us.

Wanderers

Our interfaith carpool heads home
from a humble, stronghold church.

Its members pray for all,
offering cookies, juice and social services

to those who wander in. An elder
tenders us a plate of sweets.

Many neighbors have moved on
but the pastor stays strong.

Her voice vibrates through our bones,
she's so assured.

Sister B drives home, I direct (forsaking GPS).
We've known this neighborhood for years.

Soon we're lost, though, caught
in cul-de-sacs of rubble

and crumbling homes.
At a stop sign, we stall.

Two men stride up,
lift hands to the glass,

peer in (four women, two nuns)
then vanish.

Between us: windshield,
dust swirls, vastness.

At the Vigil

When she decides to speak,
she brings along two sisters
and parks close to the door.
But the evening is soft.
They will pause and enjoy this pale, gold air,
they will enter like queens.

On stage, she fingers her scarves,
explains how she scans before entering
any street; how, in a crowd
words might flash so sharp,
she's nicked,
all for a yard of white silk,
her banner, her dove.

Silence glimmers.
She stands so still, a poplar
and holds her luminous book to her chest.
Hear her words
and feel what's beneath them:
crushed violets in the garden.

Light Perceived in Reverse

Color Wheel

My daughter asks if I can paint
all the hues that rise
between violet and green.

First, I draw a cyanometer
(De Saussure, 18th century,
tried to measure the sky).

Tracing mouths of jars, I find
a pleasing circumference
and mark intervals to fill

with washes of phthalo.
This lucent blue caresses
any paper and jumps

into full-blown affair.
When layered, it's opaque
and draws down a curtain.

De Saussure dyed paper strips
cyan, like robins' eggs
or methane, as it burns.

How do I render
another's yearning?

At dawn I hold it up
to the sky, thick with snow.
Sheets and sheets drape over yards

like closet spill.
Branches reach into white,
which is absent

of color,
but all light combined.
How I stayed up all night
to watch the circle dry,
each glowing shard,
each veil.

36

I Crave That First Kiss

of the brush on hot press
or cold press paper.
I can't afford the luxury
of thicker weaves

since I make mistakes.
And watercolor won't forget.
Each mark leaves an impression,
whispers secrets.

Winter sky lies thick
as bleached cotton rag.
It won't utter a word.
I paint spillover from dreams,

stark terrain and spectral figures.
If only air would blush
and warm the blood,
not leave me
to stumble and scratch.

Bingo Night

"Praise God in His sanctuary."
—Psalms 120

I'm wedged
between my mother and my son,
who scoot tokens on paper cards.

Voices rise when anyone enters,
as if returning from a cruise.
Willy, sit! How's the shoulder?

Static hums from hearing aids
in the humid, carpeted room.
Souls condense on windows.

We've been here two hours, postponed
the market, the shoe store. B-18, I-9
booms the mic. Praise His name!

Mom extracts cookie lumps from her purse,
scatters crumbs over our sleeves,
lifts her cheek for my son's kiss.

D-1! Someone shouts. A win!
Praise Him with lute and lyre,
with dance and drum.

Ah....flutes my son, joining
the elders, who sing out,
reedy and abundant.

Painting with Family

is a mistake,
yet I think of Monet, whose wife
carried his lunch into the garden

or Vuillard, who hid his relations
in the wallpaper, blurring edges
between pattern and form.

I could sketch
(less paraphernalia)
but foliage is thrilling,

so I mix jewel tones
while the children play tag.
A haze of green

lifts from the fields.
Fire sparks the Japanese maple.
Paint your mother! shouts Dad

from the house.
Mom startles, backlit.
Vines fling shadows, twisting

towards her.
It's a complicated pose
I could try.

She shakes her head,
waves me towards the garden
and escapes.

How We Lived

Chickens zigzag through grass,
pecking spiders and grubs,
a spirited tango.

In the kitchen, fragrance
of onions and rosemary.
The baby crawls in shadows, lunges

at her father's fingers,
sea anemones wriggling through tides.
Someone lets out the dogs

(forgot the chickens?)
Slam of doors, we sprint out
as the dogs propel

through the yard with no
rules, a game of blood lust,
legs slick in mud, wings, squawks, delicious

plunge under prickly bushes,
which saves the flock.
They huddle and breathe so softly

it's barely detectable.
It will be hours before they emerge.
We leash the dogs and pry

stickers from hair and skin
then limp inside, a mass of limbs.
The baby will remember

none of this (except, perhaps)
sea creatures glinting
in the dark kitchen, being passed

from shoulder to shoulder,
laughter and the press
of cold, flushed cheeks.

Beautiful Feet

They have beautiful feet,
smooth toes adorned with rings
polished moon colors:
pearl, yellow fat of hunter moon,
gold slivers. Girls
clang in and out of the house,
flashing bits of colored silk
like cardinals darting through brush.
They sulk in the hammock
and whisper of leaving.
I have been a good mother,
spying at arm's length.

When they leave, I will write
of my own youth,
aunts serving tea in china cups,
their hair in smooth bouffants,
discouraging breathing.
I will write of boys in cars
racing well past curfew,
air streaming, hiss
of cardinal wings,
red moon,
damp, insistent grass
trailing my toes, legs
pale as a doe's.

Obsessed

I'm obsessed with a meteorologist
on the weather channel,
the tall one, whose ears swivel
like antennae or satellite dishes
tracking low pressure systems and storms
while we sleep. He never sleeps, but endures
on spikes of humidity and tropical depressions.

Something about his voice is so familiar, so kind
and he never sets off to report from the front,
grappling with mics, tethered to cables,
whipped by waves and flying pylons,
while any sane person would evacuate,
fretful in a car on a jam-packed highway
heading out of town.

He rarely experiences weather himself.
The most light he gets comes from
the glow of computers, blipping monitors
he pours over like a bible scholar.
Perhaps he studied portents and spells,
since he speaks to me so calmly,
eyes glowing across static
on the hour and half-hour.

While cyclones and hurricane force winds
swirl in flashing yellows and greens
across the screen and into the Gulf.

While my son waits on a highway,
assuring me
the car is packed,
cell phone charged,
that he has maps.

Self-Portrait with Mirror

As I set out paints, a bird
swoops from the corner.

I should know better.
Mirrors break promises.

Propped low, they magnify
and bleach every feature.

If arranged at sharp angles,
they distort wings or faces.

Light is perceived in reverse,
delaying takeoff.

The problem with self-portrait is
focus. Mine

slips off any glassy surface.
It scans for lift off

but snags on edges
as I set down layers of glaze.

Remote Sketching

Floors below, two figures sway
under a sweltering sky
and sightless buildings.

I rough in my sketch
using soft charcoal
and agitated lines.

They seem like young boys,
wiry, nimble
as they maneuver

in traffic, weaving light
between snarling cars.
Their arms slash

like scythes,
swinging buckets
that need to be filled.

At a crosswalk, a woman
washes her chest, shirt thrown open.
She shouts to God

in an echoing voice.
How honeyed her notes,
like amber.

In the Station

I sit among echoing
foot falls, voices, calls for trains.

Gray light filters in, perfect for sketching commuters
flinging arms, clutching cups.
I open my journal, grab charcoal.

Quick, beside me, a woman
seats herself and grins, missing teeth.
Swathed in layers, she unzips a frayed canvas coat.

From one of many plastic bags, she unearths
a spiral notebook. Inside?

Drawings she shows me
of bench sleepers, men slumped in wheelchairs,
redcaps leaning on carts, faces slack.

These are not quick impressions
but studies rendered with a careful hand.

Most days she sits in this spot, she says,
walks over from the shelter. Two miles.

We eye each other.
I note the space from cheekbone to cheekbone,
from brow ridge to her chin

(as she may be doing with me)
but my train is announced.
I wave and race off, a soft scurry.

As Art

I approach the city as art.
Trains pass suburbs, flashing
windows, gray sky canvas.
This is underpainting:
tunnels, umber shadows, screech
of brakes.

Once arrived, hands
finger coats, shoulders hunch, legs
sprint up to the street.
It's a sketch, a rush of lines.

Morning tints us with patina
like bronze.
Crowds huddle on grates,
vessels lined up for the kiln.

Coats swerve down streets,
bits of bright tangerine.

I stride quickly.
Children on swings etch the sky,
scumble words. I'd linger

but must choose
my point of entry now: flat
blue doors to the hospital, the chill

definite room where my mother
lies under sheets, pale
as the first wash of the brush.

Peonies

She rides a universe of fevers,
flying carpets and white sheets.
Accordion-time billows and constricts.

When things stop rocking
she rises, stick-thin
and limps to the peonies.

My hands poise to catch her
as she snips blooms, which flinch
at such betrayal.

These are her days, sweetness
that curdles.
We wrap thick stems in flimsy cloth.

Her spine wilts and she surrenders
to a spinning bed.
Back home, I sketch these frills

she nurtured, which bruise
when touched.

Like A Fresco

Bits of our father flake off,
leaving faint impressions
of once vibrant colors.

Story lines appear and recede.
His golden retriever, his arm
stuck in a fence as a child.

Last week his eyes altered
from hazel to sky blue
(ancestors advised him in a dream.)

It's like something pure
wants to reveal itself.

He can't name me or my sisters
but is sure we're familiar, says
love as though for the first time.

Did the tribe abandon Moses
after a stroke?

Did they think he'd recall
how to navigate the stars?

Not One Word

I touch dad's shoulder and gaze
into eyes that dart like pigeons.

He won't pray, not one word,
trusts the doctors.

So I hedge bets and whisper
the wayfarer's blessing.

He calls mom every 15 minutes,
croons Sweetheart and shivers.

They keep it cool in pre-op.
I ask God for a cloak of stars

and to reignite his heart.
Last time, another man came back,

an explorer, who swerved
through hours. He'd hire cabs

to take him to the river
then forget how to swim.

Now they wheel him off.
I roam corridors

then out to the merciful street
among currents and winds

that murmur prayers,
almost recognizable.

Double Portraits

My friend strokes layers of amber
to scaffold my cheek bones.

Tracing first impressions, he trusts
his eyes will perceive

what's essential.
After twenty minutes, we switch.

He takes the model's chair
and I try to delineate

his enclosed world.
All afternoon we exchange places,

painter to model,
model to painter.

Our mentor is Bonnard,
who sketched sensation first

then followed color's logic.
Bright strokes flick across surfaces.

Dark notes also.
My friend's shirt begins to resemble

a monk's cowl. I give him
too much forehead.

Who has entered the room?

He renders me poised
to jump off the canvas.

I stare into winter. My mother
has been in hospice for weeks.

Her eyes glint from my face.
How did he see this?

Dividing Mom's Jewelry

Arrayed on her bed:
cultured pearls, pave bracelets,
brooches of flamingos and swans.

We're caught in dazzle
then glance away, as if
burned, as if fingering
stolen goods.

Some are paste,
some, flecked with rubies.
A worthy woman

girds herself.
Take these rhinestones, says one sister.
You love glitter.

Desirous, generous,
we press gold chains
into each other's arms.

Take the turquoise earrings.
You have her coloring.
She'd want this.

After the Sale

I am not of this
ancient farmhouse, not of
single pane windows,
porous to storms.

I am not of these fields
boasting of wheat,
now muffled to stubble.

I am not of this orchard
and harvesting apples,
my own belly round.

Nor of the pond,
frozen that winter our brother went sliding
in his fashionable silk coat.

Weak, yet ecstatic,
he whirled over ice
that crackled, but held.

I am not of the lawn
where our son was wed

or vistas of whirling colors,
dry leaves, deer staking claims
and the blue heron,
leaving.

Critique

I offer a drink to a friend
who studies my landscapes
strewn against a wall.

She has a clear, discerning eye
and hasn't stayed up all night,
glazing, dithering.

I'm saturated, a cloud
with no cross winds.
Nothing coalesces.

Speak the metaphor, she says,
holding up a water glass.
But I can't commit

to half-empty or half-full.
I jab a brush in sky and sea,
equal amounts

but separated.
Such a small container.
Nothing glides above or in its depths.

Exhibition

One last walk through
before the guests arrive
and I realize
        my paintings are murmuring,

exchanging motifs.
Little arrows
        zip between them.

Cumulus masses
sail from canvas to canvas
              to gallery walls
                    towards the
door.

Thick lines reach between intaglios,
tying them in knots.

Why didn't I notice?

Laughter rises near the wine and cheese table.
My images fill
        with souls

I haven't reckoned with.

Muse

For Edith Neff

Adrift in the museum,
she floats past mythic abductions,
exultations, cavorting bathers, a poet
comforting his muse.

Past weaponry and armor,
she finds an alcove near gilded Diana,
who draws her bow at the crossroads
and waits.

The great hall is cavernous, a housing
with chambers and vaulting ceilings.
She moves on, turns a corner and

comes face-to-face with Edith,
once her teacher, now

portrayed with spikes of lime and fuchsia.
Oversized, the canvas claims a wall
beside the gift shop. It's electric,

generous with texture.
Here's the studio with easel, plants and
half-dressed and unapologetic,

Edith, flourishing a brush,
gazing out of the frame, daring

anyone to comment, only enter.
            Don't linger in corners.

She'd gesture
at their tentative sketches.

            Seize space, no matter the details.

Now she lays out everything
in bold sweeps.

Somehow We Arrived

For Dorothy Corbit

That last day, we brought canvases
she could no longer see,
her gaze had receded
in scope, in horizon.

We propped them near her bed
as she composed in her mind's eye
purple hills of Morelia, adobe huts,
artists in the studio, gouaches
of orchids, lit stillness.

We stroked her brow with rough hands,
ink under our nails,
hoping to release her into waves of color.

Isn't this the way with old friends?
Love on the tongue,
brushstroke of fingers,
the heart's museum
always open.

Scatter All We've Claimed

Focus

Children toss a yellow ball across the lawn,
directing the eye.

Cousins crowd tables
of canapes and cakes.

I study this old photo, dense
as if filmed underwater.

There's tension in its depths
and leviathans are trolling,

trolling the oceans, and in the sky
plagues circle, disguised as birds,

as many winged creatures.
We gossip, sip wine and

on the green lawn,
our tender children.

Red Flags

"If you see a Spotted Lanternfly, it's
imperative to immediately report it online."
–Dept. of Agriculture

Red flags should signal caution
and do, my first sighting

of these winged bits of red
cellophane, undiluted traffic lights.

One step   trips a wire,
catapults them into sky

or back to whatever conveyed them.
But their absence

is momentary. Some wind
spirals them onto branches like confetti.

I warn neighbors, who shrug
and smile thinly

as if I prophesied UFOs.
But soon we are all

wrapping trees
with mesh and sticky traps,

trying to capture these lanterns
who hatch in the styrax, the maples,

or any surface
where they might attach

to feed and emit
their strange language.

In the Garden, Not Painting

I abandon my easel
to strike at dappled
continent jumpers, advancing

on every branch and tree trunk.
Armed with swatter and sticks,
I pry egg sacs from leaf crowns,

whatever's softhearted, smooth skinned.
These aren't woodland sprites,
they're thieves

ransacking our yards.
I smash their essence into grass
then stumble through the house.

Sleep is fitful, muddled.
I try not to dream of them
huddled under bark coverlets.

Invasive

Racing past bushes, my granddaughter
summits a log, wobbles
then falls, ignoring my open arms.

She shrieks, bends low and swats
then examines a scrawl of trembling legs
that resemble a word, mid erasure.

It flickers until she strikes again
and meets my eyes, a victor.
I chide, these are creatures

and still her soft hands
slapping at nymphs,
black and red speckles

like blood from battles, from myth.
Yes, invaders, but
what should I teach her?

Measures

I count strides
(each a foot length)
as my mother taught

to measure rugs
or the length of a room
when buying a couch.

This was years back.
Now I pace six feet
then head out, shocked

by swooping jays
and the red hat
of a neighbor, popping up

near a hedge.
He's lonely, wants to chat.
I edge back, assessing

risk, which isn't static.
Three teens jog by companionably.
One spits on the ground.

Is it safe to pass that place?
When will we find
a new way to orbit?

As They Lift

I refuse to paint one more still life
in this house, refuse

to arrange scarves or plates
piled high with fruit, to eavesdrop

on their waning conversations.
So I venture out

to witness what moves,
a line from fence edge to roof jut to

white mask of my neighbor, waving
a tentative hand.

What leads the eye, patterns?
Shadows that gesture

with bruised fingers?
Or layers, as they lift?

After Rains

Pulling on the same striped shirt each day
saves on laundry

and the birds don't care, fat robins
who skim flooded gardens.

Crows shriek warnings
then take off.

Makes no difference if I groom
or rail at storms, which scatter

all we've claimed:
trellis, fence, plantings, cracked patio

where we gathered.
I plant feet in mud.

Makes no difference if
lately, I'm more porous.

Winds snap off my hair strands,
which the birds use for nests.

Approach

The star magnolia bursts
across the street, wild
and unrepentant.
It prospers in this strange season.

It can't read the news
so it blossoms, blares out
haywire blooms, greedy fingers.

What do you reach for? I ask,
Why so cheerful?

Yet I can't resist approaching
since there's no distance
I must keep

from its triumph
in a landscape pruned
of humans.

Blue Light

Today the sky is mute.
Cumulonimbus settle
so thick and low to the ground

as to keep ghosts from rising.
I plant myself on a verge,
unfold my easel and dwell

among what's fleeting.
I grasp an old fox tail brush,
thin and bent, but

acute to branches' yearning.
Painters learn
that the sun illuminates a moment

then moves on.
Shadows cast wounds,
birches fly apart,

but I remain
as companion.
No trace of cerulean warms the sky.

I mix ochre and lavender, gray
as a dove's underbelly.
I squint and imagine blue light.

Of Glass

As weeks pass, our house
fills with breath, blood, and voice.

I make the rounds of halls
that creak like bones.

From a sepia photo, my grandmother
gazes out (queenly, serene.)

Speak! I cry,
since we once were close.

She'd play piano
and waltz us through rooms.

You must have words now
with so much unknown!

But she's placid, framed
in her palace of glass.

From sideboard to table to chair
then out into the yard, I place her

beside me on the grass, lit gold
before it dims.

Mostly I Hear Them in the Kitchen

Voices whisper they'll be here
for dinner. No need
for chairs, but please
wear the gold earrings and silk blouse,
they're so becoming.

Who will see me in them?
I won't set foot in the closet,
where hangers swing like metronomes,
like empty shoulders.

I polish candlesticks,
set out good dishes.
Shut the fridge! You'll put out an eye!

Is this from childhood,
mother shouts, I blunder
into cabinets and doors?

Now that she's gone,
I back into stories
with chipped corners.

A Landscape is Coming to Life

on a small square board
my friend props on his easel
in our yard.

He uses calm, sure strokes
to depict an arid lawn
between purple shadows.

In the center, two hollies
are wound with vines
we let flourish, a snarl.

I didn't lead him here,
didn't suggest he remain
for hours, peering

at dazzle, a vista he possesses
and now shares.
Can his view be a veil

over others?
Or will sunlight blot memory?
I often visit this spot,

which is not simple, but holy.
Once a deer sought shelter here,
bounded through landscape

and into cars, erratic,
until he was cornered
and stopped.

Capture

Starlings glide across a surface of glass
to black branches.

The view is overcast, monochrome.
I add yellow ocher for heat.

I'll catch what flies out
for memory paintings.

Later, thick strokes of varnish
(ground beetles' wings) will be applied.

This won't slow the canvas from fraying,
but may preserve what glows.

Safe Distance

We kneel yards apart,
my granddaughter and I,
pulling weeds.

She names each leaf
in her lap, leaf
on the pile, leaf.

Delighted by sound, she offers
this feast to her doll and to me, guests
at her table, this wide green lawn.

Noting birds riding wind, she cries red!
Red bird, cardinal, I expand,
feathering her nest of words.

Nearby her brother studies anthills,
intrigued by their patient construction.
He's building his own den of pebbles and sticks.

Quick! The children crawl under hedges
that bend to embrace them.

Six feet of love.
They lift arms for kisses
I can't give them.

We mime air hugs, gestures
towards each other, towards
the wind and voyaging clouds.

But as we return
to where their watchful mother stands,
they grab my fingers.

Reaching for
Shards

Else We Be Scattered

We're fabricating a mural
outside the house,
not a tower or venture
into the clouds.

This isn't hubris. We know
the earth is not of one language
and what we construct

from old toys and cracked dishes
will tell stories
no one can read completely.

It's not decoration.
We roam the city,
picking through jumble sales and trash,

rescuing soup bowls that teeter
on curbs. One family sets out
a box of ceramic amphibians.

Their son confides
they're moving in with friends and can't
keep these glowing dart frogs.

So we lug treasures back,
contorting our spines.
Will these creatures be content

to nest in shattered
shoals and tides
of our designs?

Will they add to the syllables,
phrases and words we need
to teach ourselves?

Mural

"… and all their array."
—Genesis 2:1

Cutting bone china takes strength,
but less force
                than feel.

She holds nippers
to the tile's edge, scores

then snaps it into pieces
with sharp little wheels
pressed together like the jaws

of some creature
who feeds on cups and cracked
ceramics. Reaching for shards,

she stamps feet in the cold,
spreads grout on foundation beams
which prop up the porch.

Neighbors in masks come by
to offer
            vases, wine bottles, loose beads
            from necklaces,

prismatic bits
to match broken visions

that rouse her
                in fits
and starts.

She designs in the dark,
faces the window

for a first view of dawn
and sky,
            color of grout,

becoming palpable.

75

Beautiful and Sharp

O, if she could affix
this bloodgood maple
to the mural, bright

leaves (before they fade), fingers
tipped with the latest style of lacquer,
tart mango, sweet pucker.

As she glues bits of porcelain,
leaves
            snag on jagged pieces

then release. They catch
in her collar, her hair,

release.

She chips slivers
from her mother's old cups,
favorite patterns of celadon and peach
to form tiles, edged
with sting and caress.

She asks pigeons
(hopping at her feet)
for advice.

They only coo and trill
like musical scales,
like broken rainbows.

She warns them:
don't alight
on sharp corners.

You will slip.

Apple

Should we mosaic this mottled fruit
as if it were the last?

Yes, we piece together
bud, blossom and ripeness

with squares of sap green
and crimson.

Colors vibrate side to side.
We salivate.

Grandmother's Lusters

They arrive 18 years late,
retrieved from the attic of an aunt
who claimed them as birthright

then kept them boxed.
Now I reach through layers of tissue
and hoist them, heavy as limbs,

to the upright piano.
So grandmother can play her blue waltz
at all hours, lit by ghosts,
invited guests.

My sisters claim I have space
for these bone china globes,
cinched at the waist
like bygone women.

Crystals dangle, half cracked,
half lost. They can't be repaired
so I pocket them and plan
where to place them.

Often Confounded

The mural swirls in waves
and fills
with illogical flora

from all corners of the world:
sunflowers, cacti, roses and
all they imply, all they remember.

Don't we need more sunflowers?
More roses?

The children search through their toys
for turtles and fish.
An iridescent, porcelain duck
inches forward from a shelf

so I convey her in my palm
to find the right spot.
Meanwhile, chickens peck at my feet,

real chickens, two Orpingtons
the neighbors harbor.

Fluffy and bright, they cast
such pure cobalt shadows
that I want to cry.

One fantastically plumed
yellow hen
        squawks
if her sisters turn a corner
or roost under a bush.

She's high strung
and loses them too easily.

I sing to her,
snap photos on my cell phone,
even paint her portrait in watercolors,
which doesn't calm her.

Sorting Yellow Tiles, I Remember the Deer

He sought shelter
near our fence, but couldn't
clear it with a broken leg. Shots

propel me to the window.
A large buck
shivers on his knees, facing

the source of his shock, a cop
with a rifle. They stare
at each other, then
crack, crack.

He's ocher, bright as wheat
in underbrush, attempting
to rise again and again,
all false starts.

He's done now, he's done, he was in pain,
incants the man,
who returns to his car
and grips the wheel, a statue.

Blue fog drifts down like smoke
from some ancient ritual.
I layer umber fragments over
these low lying things.

Loosen

Doves flit through sky, Mother.
I'd tie you to me.

My fingers sift beads, mostly blue,
like wavering sea stones,
your eyes.

You bequeathed this color
and elegant dresses,
discarded rings.

Ring of days.
How you curled into endless cooling,
your voice,

cloudless.

Cubist

She glues a thicket of orange slivers
to a white plate

then adds

a jagged vase of outstretched
cherry blossoms.

It's tiled and skewed, this image
so hidden

       that she feels safe.

If There Were No Whisperer

Rolling up her shirt, she
eyes us,
          glancing/glancing away

from scars
          on her forearm.

Finally, she whispers of
                    flames,
close quarters, hissing
tongues, candles
overturned.

So much
turns to bone,
bone and fire,

quick to revive.

Our fingers stiffen.

I Place a Red Tile in the Mural

for Zamir, who skipped school
after his house burned,

kitchen stove exploded, not meant
to flicker all night, warming

him and his brother, parentless
most of the winter.

We took up a collection
of clothes and spare cash.

Zamir returned, sobbing, striking out
at older boys, inviting beatings.

Followed by foster care
in another part of town,

another school.
How I miss

his gap-toothed smile, his pride
upon learning to read.

We'd hunker in back of class,
sounding things out.

Brought Forth

We separate tiles into bins:

light versus dark

warm versus cool

sea versus sky -- really,
no need to discern among

numerous greens (viridian, olive, sap, jade)

brights and mutes

silver and gold (set aside,
since grout won't hold)

fruit colors, garden colors

earth tones (for roots and roads, field creatures
who huddle and leap).

This will take months and never
be complete.

Layers

One of us loves to smash plates
then piece scraps together
like a puzzle. She trusts
where this will lead.

Another snaps on gloves
and reaches for chips, sharp
as she needs
for intricate petals, tangled thorns,
her glitter garden.

I choose from bins
or what falls,
as do the neighbor's chickens,
who peck at inspiration,

which can lead them astray.
Yesterday a woman phoned
from blocks away, perplexed
by squawking on her porch.

My art is this haphazard.
Sometimes new shapes appear overnight,
red exclamations or secrets
we notice later.

Perhaps children added them.
We welcome their fragments,
will pull this fabric
around us.

Logic I Must Learn

Comes Up April

Sap green leaves.
Plum buds, flesh
from air. We hope for

fertile gardens, fruit
of decades, haystacks
dropping from great heights.

Colors release
in new arrangements:
violet, amethyst,
scarlet lake.

Assembly

Blooms from other gardens
beckon: roses my neighbors tend,
lilies, phlox, hydrangeas,
full throated and trumpeting.

I, conversely, wear a mask
to trespass, trying
not to seem suspicious,
snapping photos for the studio,

where I will sit alone and bask,
absorbing angle, shadow,
petal and stem,
whatever echoes.

I paint without plan,
eye and hand don't
map a story line.
It's more an assembly

of bits of colored glass,
windblown shards
brushed together with logic
I must learn.

The Light Is True Today

shouts my friend
from his phone at 8 am
as he sets up his easel in a park.

It's so early that nothing stirs,
no bikes, dog walkers or wings.
Don't miss this, he advises.

A sensitive eye can predict
saturation before it begins,
can hear whispers

before leaves and buds
loosen their tongues.
I should hurry.

Sunlight can be moody,
spill quickly.
At this moment

it's a lure.
I gather my paint tubes
of ocher and cinnabar.

Taste

To everything there is
a mother, a womb.
Take this storm, a whir
in the wind. Its voice
licks clouds and cliffs.
You may not recognize
its source, a blue wish,
blackberry sweet.
Needle your tongue
for a taste.

Visiting His Studio

Because of good bones,
wide oak floors, brickwork and
low-cut rent, this old factory fills
with painters, sculptors,

bike refurbishers, fabric geniuses,
feral cats. One sits
like a barrel at the basement door,
flicking its tail, sizing me up.

An ancient freight elevator
spasms between floors,
hauling canvases, two by fours,
sheet rock, my son's table saw.

This place isn't heated.
Each one needs to warm
their own claimed space.
I prowl through a labyrinth

of hot plates, mattresses,
rag piles, propane tanks.
How will he manage in winter?
From the top of a stairwell

I weigh this life,
air like machine oil, chinks in walls,
floors so uneven,
anyone could plunge.

Space

My son planes planks,
checks for splinters.
He's building a desk with old factory salvage,
boards that once supported

machines, grime and men's weight
for so long, that now
they're as yellow as egg yolks
flecked with red.

He used to drift through parties when young,
leaving the table
to search for carved mantles,
crown moldings, curlicues and corbels.

I'd find him
stroking the grain, the artistry.
Now I bring sandwiches and
huddle near the scant warmth

of his plug-in heater.
I consider the view:
panorama, a mosaic
of high-rises and rooftops,

windows like tiles, reflecting
soft movements of humans.
I used to have
my own studio space.

I'd paint abstracts
and hold day long conversations
with crimson and ultra blue,
make marks with charcoal sticks, catch lyrics.

Painting portraits,
I'd invite souls in
to sit near the window
so they could feel a little freer.

Sun-Touch Plus

"UV-Free light. Ideal for anyone wanting to brighten their spirits."
–Nature Bright

I slant the lightbox on myself
(seasonal moods) and my palette
with its dry, little paint bluffs,

rose madder, umber, cobalt – the basics.
Also one luxury, jadeite green,
such pearly seafoam

that I lose sight of cost
and buy large tubes
to highlight

leaf tips, branches, glints
on my grandson's head.
He races through the yard with friends.

Perhaps I care too much
for jadeite, which reifies
with just a few water drops.

It seeps everywhere,
as sky blends into sea
without discernment.

Perhaps it's foolish to try
to purchase iridescence,
but I'm obsessed.

Why, on Impulse, I Bought "Bald Man with Neckerchief" by Gilbert Lewis

Because of bold brushwork and flawless
placement of the model in space,

that piratical look and red neckerchief.
Because the gallery owners love this piece,

displayed far back from window glare.
And galleries like this are rare.

Because last month I sold enough watercolors
to cover the cost.

I can't paint with such mastery,
but hang it in my studio like a shrine.

Did you notice the asymmetry of the eyes?
One, shaded; one, a jaunty gaze

at the painter.
What was their relationship?

Was this really an impulse,
or was I pulled to the energy and verve

of all those beautiful young men
he painted in the 70s and 80s, despite

AIDS, despite
meager interest in portraits (then or now)?

My brother would have bought one
had he lived.

My brother, who was
this stylish, this elegant.

My Students Write Lists

of animals, collections
in backpacks or desks.
Mysteries, family names,
acts of bravery, desserts,
one brave thing they did last week,
something remembered or lost.

The room fills with plush
dinosaurs and bears. I reel back
to T-rex bits hiding in socks,
biting our heels. They stung
but my brother, beautiful boy,
leapt over spiked tails
and never drew blood.

I polish my inventory
like it's a resume:
marriages, new houses, nieces
and nephews (one bears his name.)
In my daughter's house
his portrait keeps watch
over her children, stacking blocks
into cities, hiding, dancing.

Family Portrait

We sit at intervals on the porch,
masked, but still a family
passing challah, pre-sliced.

No tearing the loaf,
no fingering shiny crust
before sharing.

The youngest, learning language,
invents a game.
She grasps the top page

from a colorful stack
on her father's knee.
Rounding the table,

she slaps lilac on her mother's lap.
Returns.
Selects a square of aqua for me.

Returns.
Chooses peach for one sister,
jade green for another,

orange for her grandfather.
Is she mapping Sabbath?
Weaving us in?

Each departure/arrival,
each circuit of the table
is met with cheers.

Does she realize we're smiling?
The muscles of our cheeks and lips
are hidden.

Yes! affirms the oldest child.
She sees lines of kindness
around our eyes.

Sparks and Disperses

The house is an ark,
rain pounds the hull.

Sparks scatter,
dispersing cerulean storms.

We scratch out questions and riddles
in the language of hawks:

What drives the red ocher fox from the garden?
How long can a whale hold its breath?

Winds croon of ancient seas, withdrawn.
We sing with centrifugal force.

Someday, when the children search for maps,
they'll find what we invented.

One, a Tiger

One in a wizard's costume,
one, a queen
one, a tiger.

Children race through the house
shrieking like sirens,
tying us up in spells.

The youngest circles and yowls
until caught in our arms.

We nuzzle her cape and sharp sequins.
She brandishes her wand, demands

to be let down,
let loose.

The Children Sequester Themselves

inside a castle
of cardboard blocks
in our dim basement.

They war sometimes,
roar chest to chest
and steal each other's toys

until we make them
fold up the tigers,
the warriors, the hawks.

So it was with their parents
long afternoons ago, snowbound,
temps below zero

and all of us, desirous
of any dark space
to launch into.

Naming

My daughter and her wife rescued
                              a tomcat
to companion the sweet, aged female
who prowls through their house.

Asa, our grandchild (age 4)
named the cat
              Guiseppe
then declared it
              a girl.

Lately we've been crawling
beside the felines
comparing their underbellies
with reference photos.

But Asa insists
              as if
enlightened in a dream.

He says
        Giuseppe will tell us

she's a girl
when she's older.

My Grandchild and I Dream on the Couch

Her breath beats so fast,
like a bird's under my hands,
which span her ribs.

She is so delicate, so fierce,
just four days old.
She whimpers, recounts
her journey to us.

I soothe with calm, quick strokes
and murmur like a river.

Prayers are prescribed
for the fear and joy of this moment
and I've said them

in the hospital, as risks
were tallied
then tamped down.

I whisper secrets, predictions
only we will hear.
I add a stitch to her comfort cloth.

If, someday, she rocks her own grandchild,
I'll be gone.

My voice?
A swirl in the air, soft
but there.

She Appears

Sporting backpack, green dinosaur
boots, brother's fleece bear cap,
a spoon, a muffin tin.

Throwing open the door,
she grabs me for leverage,
hops downstairs.

Backpack drops
(too furry, too loose). Rage
throws her onto pavement.

She weeps and won't be calmed
until returned to herself, new

and prone to slip.
At the corner I grasp her

though chimeras can't wait,
borne as they are by storms.

Finally reaching the park,
she receives her due, applause

for magnificent fur
and reptile ankles.

She staggers to the top of the slide
and roars.

Dust

I abandon my desk, twist
down the stairwell and out
to the street into a nearby church,

which hosts Tibetan monks,
three saffron-robed men
bent over the floor, scattering

colored sand. I blink
to adjust to dim space.
Why don't they ask for more light?

Two weeks they've been here,
intent on their artwork.
Static fills the chapel.

Are they whispering? Praying?
Or is this the rasp of their sticks
dispersing dust?

Oceans form storms,
fanciful creatures, desires, all
needing to be noticed or made pure.

Fringed flowers, vines, yellow tongues,
secret doors. I often return,
but can't bring myself

to that last ritual, that final day.
I hear that local children arrive
and bring brooms.

Everyone stands in a circle and chants
until one monk breaks
the mandala with his thumb.

This signals a great collecting of dust
into jars, carried to the river and cast.
To widen the blessing.

Acknowledgments

This collection is dedicated to Tiffany Silliman Cohen and Rabbi Gila Colman Ruskin, who invited me to join them in creating a beautiful mural. Gratitude to Nathalie Anderson, Katherine Barham, and Alyson Adler for their knowledge and poetry expertise.

The poems in this collection make reference to many inspiring people (both alive and departed). Among them: Jean Alexander, Huda Aziz, Abigail Bialer, Joe Brenman, Dorothy Corbit, Shahbanu Goldberg, Nancy Golieb, Adab Ibrahim, Fadwa Kashkash, Blew Kind, Connie, Harvey, Liz and Peter Krueger, Tilda Mann, Edith Neff, Sr. Beverly Palumbo, and Jeff Thomsen. Thanks to many students, artists, writers, educators and advocates for children whom I've been fortunate to work with. To highlight a few: the entire Artwell community, Ilon Bavli, Jihad El-Sana, Sanaa Abu Asbah Watad, Steve Shapiro and AHED High School for Science, Cerulean Arts Gallery, and RitualWell.

What a pleasure and honor it has been to work with Cornerstone Press. It is impressive to experience this team's professionalism, collaboration, and creativity. Special thanks to Dr. Ross K. Tangedal, Director & Publisher; Kyra Goedken, Director of Operations; Gavrielle McClung, Editor-in-Chief; Kala Buttke, Managing Editor; and Alexander Soukup, Production Director and Cover Designer.

I am grateful for support and inspiration from my wonderful friends and family, especially Adam, Alex, Asa, Gabrielle, Jordan, Juliet, Madeleine, Rachel, Tiffany, and Willa. Love and gratitude to my husband, David.

* * *

Gratefully acknowledged are the editors from the following journals and publications in which particular poems first appeared:

"Why I Paint at Dawn", published in *30 Days of Inspiration* (online, Arts & Cultural Council of Bucks County); "Pomegranate", published in *6ix*; "Writing Poems in Beersaba'h", published in *Storm Cycle* (Kind of a Hurricane Press); "Ink Drawings", published in *6ix* (as 'T'ai Chi'); "Equations", published in *Voices for Diversity and Social Justice* (Rowman & Littlefield); "Shimmer Around Us", published in *Apiary Magazine*; "Bingo Night", published in *Poetica Magazine*; "Beautiful Feet", published in *The Breath of Parted Lips* (CavanKerry Press); "Obsessed", published in *Baltimore Review*; "In the Station", published in *Schuylkill Valley Journal*; "As Art", published in *Rockvale Review*; "Invasive", published in *Bindweed*; "Measures", published in *North of Oxford* (online); "After Rains" and "Approach", published in *Virus* (Moonstone Press); "Safe Distance", published in *Global Poemic*; "Mostly I Hear Them in the Kitchen", published in *Voices of the Grieving Heart* (Cypress Point Press); "Mural", published in *Beir Bua* (online); "Space", published in *One Art Journal* (online); "Family Portrait", published in *RitualWell* (online, as "Pandemic Sabbath"); "One, a Tiger", published in *Chrysalis* (online); "Naming", published in *Passager*.

CATHLEEN COHEN was the 2019 Poet Laureate of Montgomery County, Pennsylvania. A painter and teacher, she founded the We the Poets program at ArtWell, an arts education non-profit in Philadelphia (theartwell.org).

Her poems appear in journals such as *Apiary*, *Baltimore Review*, *Cagibi*, *East Coast Ink*, *6ix*, *North of Oxford*, *One Art*, *Passager*, *Philadelphia Stories*, *Rockvale Review*, and *Rogue Agent*. *Camera Obscura* (chapbook, Moonstone Press), appeared in 2017, and *Etching the Ghost* (Atmosphere Press), was published in 2021.

She received the Interfaith Relations Award from the Montgomery County PA Human Rights Commission and the Public Service Award from the National Association of Poetry Therapy. Her paintings are on view at the Cerulean Arts Gallery (ceruleanarts.com).